Here Come the Heebie Jeebies

and other Scary Poems

compiled by Tony Bradman

Illustrated by David Roberts

HODDER Wayland

an imprint of Hodder Children's Books

Here Come the Heebie-jeebies

We are the heebie-jeebies
We live beneath your bed
We like to give you nightmares
With our teeth and eyes all red

We are the heebie-jeebies
Hear us howl and moan
We like to pay you visits
When you're all alone

We are the heebie-jeebies
Monsters, giants, ghouls
We wait for you to fall asleep
We're very mean and cruel

So here come the heebie-jeebies
Prepare to get a fright...
But... you wouldn't do that, would you?
DON'T TURN ON THAT LIGHT!

Tony Bradman

Lost in Woolworths

Oh, no! I'm lost in Woolworths!
My mum's nowhere in sight!
She was buying me new plimsoles
(my old ones are too tight).

She was over by the checkout.
I was at the Pic 'n' Mix
But now she's gone and vanished
And I'm in an awful fix.

Oh, the panic! Oh, the horror!
Oh, the heat, the noise, the crowd!
I think I might start crying,
And I think It might be LOUD!

WAAAAAAAAAAAAAAH!

Then, joy of joys! I see her!
With my plimsoles in a packet.
"Oh, there you are! Where have you been?
And what's that awful racket?"

I take her hand. I smile a bit.
She buys me Juicy Fruits.
And everything's all right again –
'Til I get lost in Boots!

Kaye Umansky

Voices in My Head

I daren't!
You can do it.
I can't
You can do it.
What if...?
You can do it.
Perhaps...
You can do it.
DARE I do it?
You can do it.
Well, MAYBE I should...
You can do it.
I DID IT!
I said you could do it.
I knew I would!

Judith Nicholls

You can do it . . .

My Crocodile

My Crocodile is very small.
He has no claws or teeth at all.
He doesn't scratch.
He doesn't bite
He's safe to take to bed at night.

I love his little beady eyes.
I love him more than lullabies.
I love his cheeky crockish grin.
So don't forget to tuck him in.

For when he's there, I'm glad to say,
He helps to snap bad dreams away.

Tony Mitton

Little Horse in the Wardrobe

Tap of hooves like clothes-hangers chiming
then a whinny that might be
the shut-down of the central heating

or a horse calling to me,
the chink of its harness like coins
loose in my jeans.

Little horse, I whisper
and he answers
with the smart spark of his metal shoes.

This is a bad place for you
all big buildings and cars
nowhere you can put down your head
and eat grass.

Stay where you are,
I whisper. It's better
for you in the dark where

your eyes shine bright
as you make pictures of what might
be waiting for
little horses
out there.

Helen Dunmore

Fear

I'd rather be caught by a python,
I'd rather be covered in fleas,
I'd rather be eaten by spiders
or boy-eating sharks in the seas

I'd rather be chased by a monster
melted alive by the sun
eat bogies, and earwax forever, than:
be kissed in the playground by Mum.

Peter Dixon

Please, Mr Dentist...

Please be gentle with my teeth.
I may look tough, but underneath
I'm trembling like an autumn leaf,
and it would be a great relief
if you didn't look at them today.
I'll come when you're less busy... say
next week, next year, when I'm forty-five
(that's if we're both still alive).
I'll brush them twenty times a day
if you'll just let me get away.

I wouldn't really mind a filling
if it wasn't for the drilling.
I've heard its nasty grinding noise.
Oh won't you put away your toys:
those shiny metal bits and bobs
you like to poke in people's gobs?

I like your clean white coat and smile.
How nice to stay and chat a while.
I wouldn't mind one tiny bit
the fizzy pinkish rinse-and-spit.
I love the tilty-backwards chair,
but this is more than I can bear...

What's that? It's over? I can go?
I wasn't really scared, you know.
My teeth are fine today? That's great.
See you in six months' time then, mate!

Jean Sprackland

Meeting the Snake

I used to fear you,
slithery snake,
the way you move,
the shapes you make.

But now I've met you
at the zoo,
I've changed the way
I think of you.

I used to think you
slippy, sly.
And yet I find you
clean and dry,

and soft and slow
and good to touch.
So now I do not fear you,
much.

Tony Mitton

Bottling it Up

If you bottle up
your worries and fears.
Bottle them up for years
and years. They'll slowly
fill you to the top.
Until one day
you'll just go

POP!

And every single scary feeling,
will be splattered across
the kitchen ceiling.
So save the mess,
admit you are scared!
Worries get smaller
when they are shared!

Mandy Coe

Step by Step

(to be read from bottom to top)

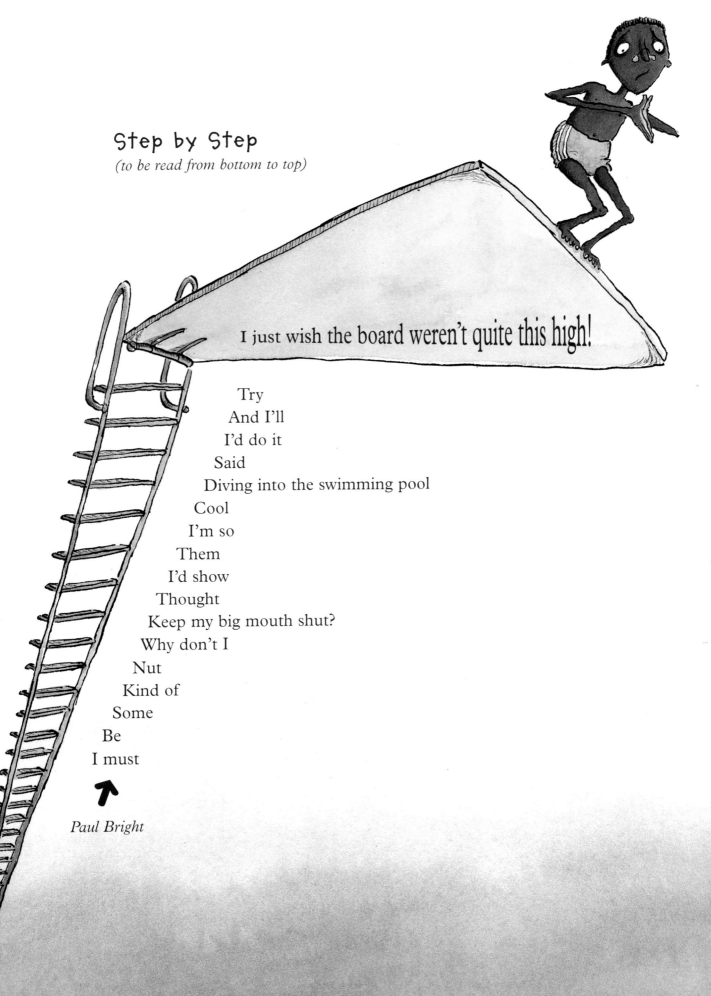

I just wish the board weren't quite this high!

Try
And I'll
I'd do it
Said
Diving into the swimming pool
Cool
I'm so
Them
I'd show
Thought
Keep my big mouth shut?
Why don't I
Nut
Kind of
Some
Be
I must

Paul Bright

The Best Film Ever

Did you see that film on telly last night?
It nearly gave my mum a fit,
Especially when that ghastly green horror
Came dripping out of the pit.

Then there's that really awful bit
(You know I hate things that slither)
When they hauled this great squid up out of the sea
And you saw it die and wither.

I've not even mentioned the Egyptian mummy,
Or Frankenstein, or the yeti;
Oh yes, there was this mad professor too —
He terrified our Aunt Betty.

Afterwards it took our family ages
To pull itself together,
But after cups of cocoa all round
We voted it The Best Film Ever.

Eric Finney

The Heroes

You never saw anything
Quite so brave,
As my (little) brother Harry
And his friend Dave.

Harry waves a sword,
Dave bangs a spear,
They march and they chant.
It's quite a thing to hear.

Grandma's House is Scary

Grandma's house is scary,
not very nice at all.
There's an oojamaflip in her kitchen
and a wotsit in her hall.
There's a doo-da on the landing,
and a thingummy under the bed.
At least, that's what Grandma said.
Mummy says I'm silly,
that it's just Grandma's way,
of saying things she can't remember,
"so run along and play".
But I think Mummy's fibbing,
so I won't get in their way.

When I go to Grandma's,
I say a little prayer,
that the oojamaflip won't get me
and the wotsit won't be there.
I don't go up the staircase,
in case the doo-da is about
and I won't go near the bedroom,
in case the thingummy jumps out.

Marie Murray

The Ghost of Classroom Three

There's a tapping at the window,
A moaning at the door,
And something ectoplasmic
Sticking to the floor...

But don't panic, don't be frightened
By anything you see,
It's really nothing special,
Just the ghost of classroom three.

It doesn't come out often,
Maybe once or twice a year.
It wanders around and mutters,
then...poof! It disappears.

Sometimes it sits at the desk
Marking books continually...
But it's really nothing special,
Just the ghost of classroom three.

Some say it was a teacher
Who met a nasty end...
She had a class of awful kids
Who drove her round the bend.

And sometimes there is screaming,
And it weeps dismally...
But it's really nothing special,
Just the ghost of classroom three.

She swore she'd come and haunt them,
But they laughed and didn't care,
And now she haunts the cupboard
(Which otherwise is bare).

And sometimes there are others,
A whole classful you can see.
Doing endless homework
For the ghost of classroom three.

Some say it isn't possible,
And that it's just a story...
But classroom three, you must admit,
Feels different... sort of eerie.

And once, upon the blackboard
Someone wrote mysteriously,
"I'll haunt this school forever...
I'm the ghost of classroom three."

There's a rapping on the desk tops,
There's a rattling at the door,
And something trying to get out
of teacher's locked desk drawer...

But don't panic, don't be frightened,
don't scare too easily;
It's really nothing special;
Just the ghost of classroom three...

Tony Bradman

The Thing

See the teacher reel with horror!
Hear the children squeal and scream!
Watch them all retreat in terror,
From The Thing that's not a dream!

Listen to the slimy sliding!
See The Thing emerge some more!
Feel the panic, watch them hiding
Could they make it to the door?

Is The Thing an alien creature?
Is that why the classroom froze?
No... "Get a tissue!" said the teacher.
The Thing had come... from Jason's nose!

Tony Bradman

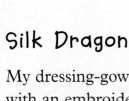

Silk Dragon

My dressing-gown was white and made of silk
with an embroidered dragon on the back.
He had a dark-blue spiralled twisting tail
and pale-blue fangs sharp in his open mouth.
During the day, he hung behind the door
but every night, just as I closed my eyes,
he left the cloth and slid into the dark
and empty spaces underneath my bed.
And so I told my mum how scared I was
in case he scorched me with his fire-breath.
She said she'd take my dressing-gown away.
I felt much better then, but later on
after she'd gone, and it was dark again
I realized how flat he could become:
a long, thin, dragon-ribbon of blue silk
slithering silently beneath the door.
The landing-light would stop him. I knew that,
and told my mum so, fifty years ago.

I still keep one small lamp on through the night.

Adèle Geras

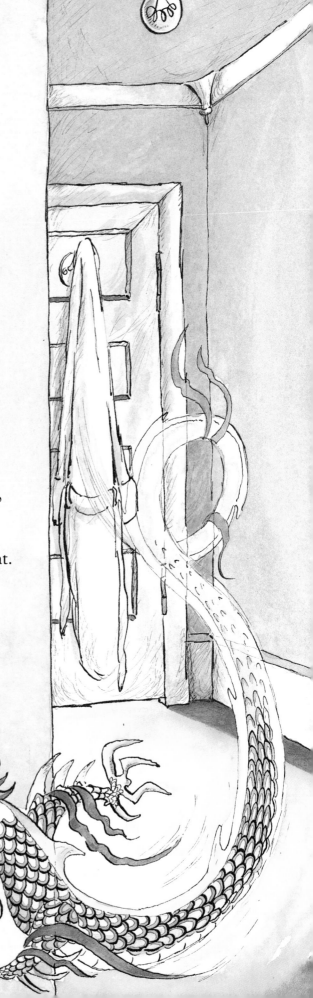

I'm not Scared of the Monster

I'm not scared of the monster
That hides beneath my bed.
When it leaps out
To prowl about,
I pat it on the head.

I'm not scared of the monster
That lurks behind the door.
When it leaps out
To prowl about,
I shake its furry paw.

I'm not scared of the monster
That sulks under the chair.
When it leaps out
To prowl about,
I stroke its spiky hair.

I'm not scared of the monsters,
'Cause they're no longer there.
When I leapt out
To scream and shout,
I gave them all a scare!

John Foster

Going Upstairs

Only the bravest person dares
To go up the trickety, rickety stairs.

The first step creaks like a bending bone.
On the second there's a stain.
You have to miss the third step out
Or you'll never come down again.

Hold your breath on the fourth step.
On the fifth step count to five.
Close your eyes on the sixth step
Or you'll never come down alive.

Only the bravest person dares
To go up the trickety, rickety stairs.

Left foot on the seventh,
On the eighth your right.
Once you reach the ninth step
Your bedroom door's in sight.

Safely on the landing
Keep a steady head:
Cross you fingers as you go and...
Jump into bed.

      Phew!

Celia Warren

How Scary!

I'm frightened of my shadow
And I'm frightened of the dark;
I'm frightened, too, of next-door's dog,
Or of being eaten by a shark;
But what gets REALLY SPOOKY,
As I'm sure you will agree,
Is when I give a little burp –
And the TEACHER KNOWS it's me!

Trevor Harvey

First Day

First day,
School gate,
Hope I'm
Not late.
Strange kids,
Fun and play,
I want to
Run away.
So scared,
Want my mum,
When, then
Will she come?
No one
Speaks to me,
Can't wait
'Til half-three.
Boy laughs,
Says Hi!
My smile,
Big as sky!
At break,
Hide and Seek,
Best fun,
All week.
In class,
Dream and draw,
Then play
Some more.
First day,
Yakkety-yak,
Can't wait to
Come back!

Andrew Fusek Peters

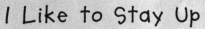

I Like to Stay Up

I like to stay up
and listen
when big people talking
jumbie stories

I does feel
so tingly and excited
inside me

But when my mother say
"Girl, time for bed"

Then is when
I does feel a dread

Then is when
I does jump into me bed

Then is when
I does cover up
from me feet to me head

Then is when
I does wish I didn't listen
to no stupid jumbie story

Then is when
I does wish I did read
me book instead.

Grace Nichols

Tony Bradman and Hodder Wayland would like to thank the following for contributing to this collection:

Here Come the Heebie-jeebies © Tony Bradman 2000
Lost in Woolworths © Kaye Umansky 2000
Voices in My Head © Judith Nicholls 2000
My Crocodile © Tony Mitton 2000
Little Horse in the Wardrobe © Helen Dunmore 2000
Fear © Peter Dixon 2000
Please Mr Dentist... © Jean Sprackland 2000
Meeting the Snake © Tony Mitton 2000
Bottling it Up © Mandy Coe 2000
Step by Step © Paul Bright 2000
The Best Film Ever © Eric Finney 2000
The Heroes © Emily Smith 2000
Miss More © Linda Allen 2000
Shadow © Gina Douthwaite 2000
White Knuckle Ride © Jane Clarke 2000
Grandma's House is Scary © Marie Murray 2000
The Ghost of Classroom Three © Tony Bradman 1989
The Thing © Tony Bradman 2000
Silk Dragon © Adèle Geras 2000
I'm Not Scared of the Monster © John Foster 2000
Going Upstairs © Celia Warren 2000
How Scary! © Trevor Harvey 2000
First Day © Andrew Fusek Peters 2000
I Like to Stay Up © Grace Nichols 1988

PILLGWENLLY

26-07-18

ELIN	
Z774965	
PETERS	26-Aug-2011
821.008	£4.99